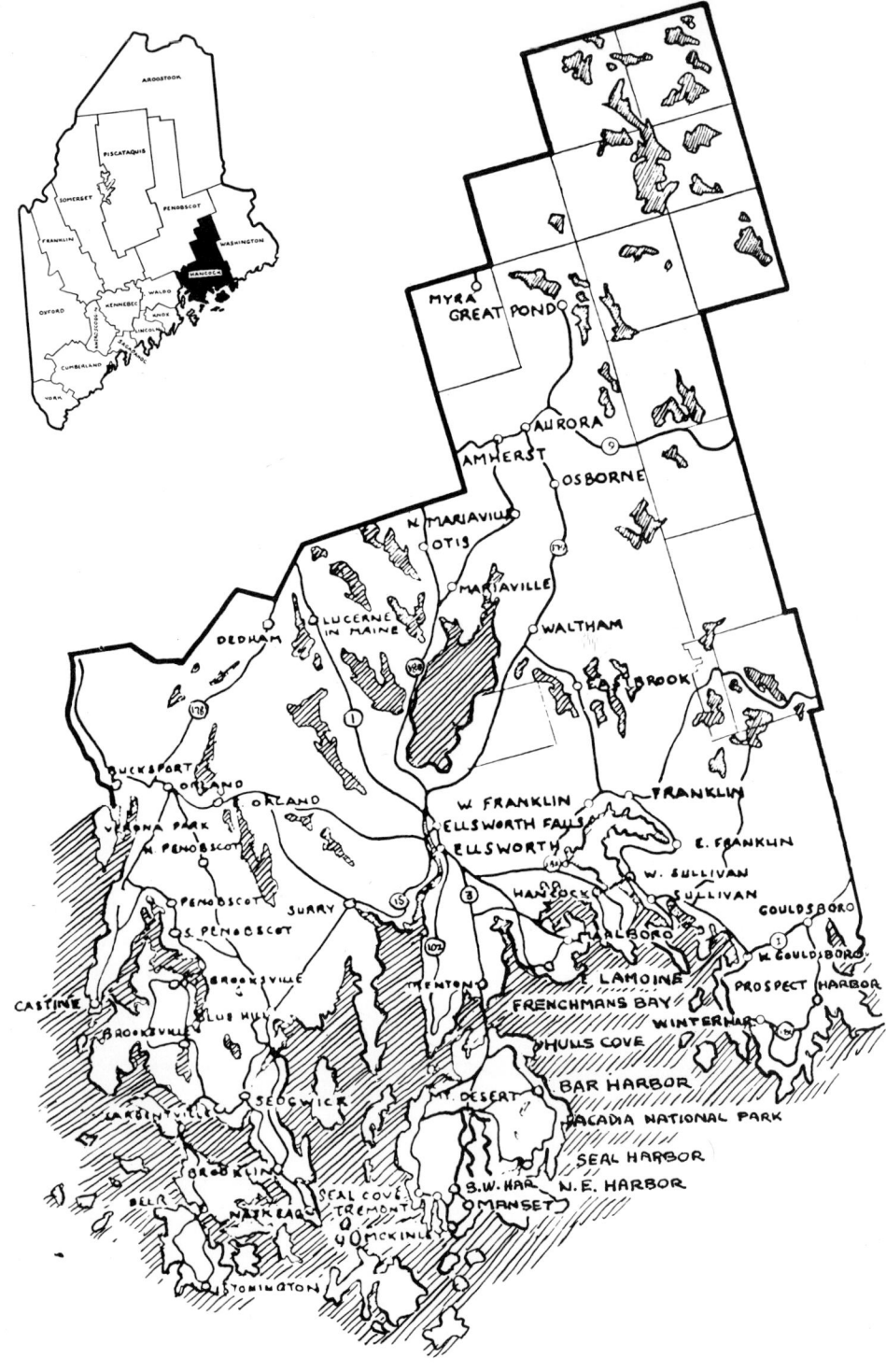

ILLUSTRATED COUNTY EDITION

MAINE PLACE NAMES
and
THE PEOPLING OF ITS TOWNS

by

AVA HARRIET CHADBOURNE

Foreword by Elizabeth Ring

Hancock

The Bond Wheelwright Company

Freeport, Maine

Copyright 1957 by Ava Harriet Chadbourne
New illustrated edition:
Copyright 1970 by Cumberland Press Inc.
Library of Congress Catalog Card No. 77-115159
SBN 87027-112-1
Manufactured in the United States of America
In Canada:
Abelard-Schuman Canada Ltd., Ontario

County map adapted from one appearing in the Maine Register, by special permission of the Fred L. Tower Cos.

We are very grateful to Vernal Hutchinson, author of A Maine Town in the Civil War, who helped us to obtain photographs from the majority of the sources used in this volume.

PICTURE CREDITS

Bar Harbor Historical Society: bottom page 26; pages 28, 30
Bridges, Susan F.: bottom page 5; page 6; top page 8
Brooklin Historical Society: page 56
Brooksville Historical Society: pages 46, 47
Bucksport Historical Society: bottom page 17; pages 18, 19, 20, 21, 22, 24; top page 32   cover
Davis, Gerald F.: bottom page 32; pages 33, 34, 35, 36, 37, 38, 39, 41, 42
Deer Isle-Stonington Historical Society: pages 10, 60
Grant, Lyndon: pages 3, 4; top page 5; bottom page 8; 9
Martin, Alfred G.: page 50
Smith, Emeline K.: top page 17
Wilson Museum, Castine: top page 26

Foreword

*There was world enough then,
and more time than there is now*
David Brower

Maine Place Names and the Peopling of Its Towns, written with feeling and a love for Maine, was for the author a rewarding endeavor of a life spent in piecing together the scattered records of the state — for others, a simple explanation of how towns came to be. If it is a reminder of the courage of those who preceded us in the mastery of their natural surroundings, so too is it a suggestion that in a more complex world today, problems of environmental control of a different nature await solution by another generation, many of whom are descendants of the old.

Local history is grass-roots history, and here it is in "the peopling of its towns," for this is both the land and the names of those who pushed into it, the settlers who gave it birth, who named the mountains and lakes and rivers, the nubbles and islands, as well as the political divisions that made it up. It was a land unpolluted by anything other than what nature in the course of time might have done in its own capricious way. And these were the people who built the white houses along the village green, the churches and academies that graced the landscape seen by later generations in the first flush of motoring as they rode over the unsurfaced roads to discover the state anew.

These towns in Maine were of all ages. Some dated from the early seventeenth century before the Massachusetts Bay colony took over to save the godless from perdition. Settlements grew slowly. Men were loath to come to a hostile land marked by the cruelty of Indian uprisings as the English fought the French and Indians in the struggle for a continent. After 1763 more rapid settlement set in as hardy pioneers in the more populated areas to the south moved to the northern outposts along the Maine coast and thence into the interior to form the second and third tier of towns as the frontier advanced.

In the building of towns there was a sameness as settlements fell into pattern. Loghouses became framehouses, paths cut through the wilderness became road, and planks thrown over creeks became bridges.

Mill sites sprang to life. Logs were sawn into timber, and wool was carded into cloth. Townships lotted by proprietors after the tedious "running of the line" by chainmen, became plantations, and plantations became towns, until, in three centuries, Maine had passed through all the stages of a frontier and the public domain had passed to private ownership.

And now in all this history combined with the natural beauty of the state there is magic for the tourist. Despoilers of the coastline and countryside are met by the closed ranks of an aroused citizenry who hold in trust that which generations before have built. "There was world enough then, and more time than there is now."

Elizabeth Ring

NOTE: This is one of a series of sixteen books — one for each county of Maine — using Ava Chadbourne's original text and adding as many old photographs as we could find or have room for within this volume's format. We realize there are many sources of picture material we have not been able to tap, but we hope to keep adding photographs to our collection for each county and at a future date to do a more thorough picture survey of the entire state.

We are most grateful to all those who have contributed to this volume, and though in some instances there is a disproportionate number of pictures for an area, we hope you, the reader, will assist us in rounding out this survey of Maine by lending us any photographs you may have of areas neglected in this volume. If you know of a picture source we might seek out, we would be delighted to hear of it. If you can make an important, authenticated addition to Miss Chadbourne's text, be sure to send a picture to go with it, and we will do our best to insert it in the next edition.

The Editor

HANCOCK COUNTY
1789

When the divisional line was made between Lincoln and Hancock counties, it left to Lincoln the sea coast between the New Meadows and Penobscot bays and all the adjacent islands. The eastern boundary of Hancock County has already been noted as the western boundary of Washington County. Hancock County, like Washington, was bounded on the north "by the utmost northern limits" of the state, and the opposite islands were also annexed. When Hancock County was being established, John Hancock, one of the most eminent men of the Commonwealth, was governor. He died in office in 1793. During this time, Maine, which had been made a maritime district in 1778, was reconfirmed as a District in 1790.

Penobscot, 1787

The name of this town, the only one in Hancock County which has Indian origin, is taken from that of the river and bay upon which it is located. Originally used for that section of the river between Treat's Falls at Bangor and the Great Falls at Old Town, the word is best translated as "the rocky part" or "the descending ledge place."

The town of Penobscot was the first town to be organized on the eastern bank of the Penobscot waters in 1787. At that time it embraced the celebrated peninsula of Castine and the eastern part of Brooksville. It was township No. 3 in the conditional grant to David Marsh and others given by the General Court in 1762, an effectual settlement having been started two years before by eight or ten families migrating across the bay from the neighborhood of Fort Pownal.

The names of those coming in 1761 have been given as Joseph Basteen, Paul and Caleb Bowdoin, John Connor, John Grindle, Archibald Haney, who later went to Brooksville, Thomas Wescott and Israel Veazie. In the confirmation of titles, the Jarvis brothers, who were large landholders, had a prominent agency.

The first survey of the town was made by John Peters; the first settlers within the present limits of Penobscot were Duncan and Findley Malcolm, Daniel and Niel Brown. They were Scotsmen and being Loyalists, left for St. Andrews when the English evacuated Castine at the close of the Revolutionary War.

The first permanent settler was Chas. Hutchings, in 1765. In that same year came Isaac and Jacob Sparks, Daniel Perkins, Samuel Averill and Solomon Littlefield. Others of the early period were Giles Johnson, Elijah Winslow, Pelatiah Leach, Jonathan Wardwell and Elipalet Lowell, nearly all of whom came from towns in Maine. The plantation name for Penobscot was Major-bigwaduce, which, according to the late Mrs. Eckstorm, is an Abenaki word meaning "a big tidal salt bay" referring to the whole so-called Bagaduce River, not merely to Castine Harbor.

The soldiers from Fort Pownal who came to our present town of Penobscot at an early date and often did not remain permanently, sent petitions from time to time to the General Court for land where they wanted to be settlers.

In 1779 Aaron Banks, after his home was burned at the siege of Bagaduce, moved to the head of Northern Bay and settled in what is now Penobscot. He was born in York, Maine, enlisted in the French and Indian war under Captain James Cargill and was ordered to assist in building Fort Pownal. He then went to Castine (Bagaduce), and was transferred for service under General Amherst to Montreal in 1760. He was discharged in 1764 and walked to York, Maine. He then married and returned to Bagaduce, and became a successful farmer, sometimes engaged in navigation. He became a permanent settler in our present Penobscot. Andrew Herrick, Nathaniel Veazie and Andrew Wescott arrived at an early date, as well as Timothy Blake, Joseph Lowell, Nathaniel, Jonathan, Jeremiah and Abraham Stover, Benj. Curtis, Benjamin and Edward Howard and Andrew Webster: all of this latter group about 1762.

Sedgwick, 1788

Major Robert Sedgwick of Charleston, Massachusetts, a man of popular manners and military talents and a onetime member of the celebrated artillery company in London, and Captain John Leverett of Boston, a correct tactician and enthusiastic patriot, were placed in command of an expedition of 500 men whom Cromwell had directed to reduce the Dutch colony at Manhadoes. Before the expedition was ready to depart, articles of peace were signed between the English and Dutch colonies.

The eastern inhabitants greatly feared the Indians and the French control over them. Cromwell's orders to the captains of the ships before they left England were, when they had reduced the Dutch colony, to turn their arms against Nova Scotia and conquer it. No time was lost in carrying out these orders whereby Major Sedgwick

Top: The village blacksmith. Sedgwick
Bottom: The stage coach. Sedgwick in the nineties

Top: The country school. Sedgwick
Bottom: The schooner "Hope Gower" launching 10/13/82. Sargentville (Sedgwick)

Top: The Town Hall on the hill. Sedgwick a century ago
Bottom: House afire, 1912. Sedgwick volunteer firemen apparently had to use a bucket line for this one.

Top: Jim Snow and his butcher cart. Sedgwick
Middle: Uphill and down dale--Town House Road. Sedgwick
Bottom: Steamboat wharf, 1910, with the Eastern S.S.Co. "Juliette" at the dock.
   Sedgwick

captured the three key fur trading posts at Pentagoet (Castine), St. John (Jemsac) and Port Royal (Annapolis Royal). Cromwell granted Acadia to Colonel Sir Wm. Temple, who carried on the monopoly of the fur trade until 1667.

It is from Major Robert Sedgwick that the town of Sedgwick, Maine, received its name in 1788. The place had previously been called Naskeag, an Indian name meaning "the extremity" or "the tip." Sedgwick was one of the six townships or No. 4 in the first class granted by Massachusetts in 1761 to David Marsh and 359 others. These townships were to be six miles square and located contiguously between the Penobscot and Union rivers.

The first permanent settler in Sedgwick was Andrew Black in 1759. Four years later came Captain Goodwin Reed, John and Daniel Black, and two years after them Reuben Gray moved in from Penobscot. His descendants are very numerous. In 1789 the court confirmed to each settler 100 acres of land. The first minister of Sedgwick was Daniel Merrill. The Town Hall, a handsome white structure on a hill overlooking the village, was built as a church in 1837 to replace the first church which was built in 1794. Four columns ornament the front entrance and a weather vane surmounts the attractively domed cupola. Daniel Merrill, first pastor of the church, received an annual salary of 50 pounds.

That the town was not particularly prosperous in the early days is shown by the official records which reveal that all unattached and unmarried females who could not find anyone to undertake their support were warned to leave town. Among the estates of first settlers in Hancock County which were appraised from 1787 to 1792 were those of John Gray and Nathaniel Allen, Sedgwick, Daniel Bridges and Andrew Black.

About eighty heads of families are mentioned as in Sedgwick in the census of 1790. Among them, in addition to names mentioned above, were Herrick, Freathy, Gra, Billings, Grindel, Dodge, Allen, Fly, Cozens, Wells, Eaton, Carter, Parker, Mahoney, Reed, Bunker, Hooper, Black and Stanley.

Bluehill, 1789

Mary Ellen Chase, in her delightful book, *Jonathan Fisher, Maine Parson*, quotes the following from some early descriptive sketches written by this clergyman who settled here in 1796. In these he explains the reason for the naming of the town:

About 1½ miles from the harbor, there rises to the north a hill which is 950 feet above high water mark. The as-

Top: The boat wharf, Sargentville (Sedgwick), with Eastern S.S. Co. "J. T. Morse" at the dock.
Bottom: The copper mine. Bluehill, 1880. (Note: though Miss Chadbourne spelled this town as above and it was so spelled in the late 19th century, the correct spelling now is Blue Hill.)

Top: Bluehill about a century ago
Bottom: The first Bluehill fair

Top: A nineteenth century tractor, at Deer Isle. Carmen's Rock in left background
Bottom: The main street of Northwest Harbor in 1884. Deer Isle

cent to the rocky summit is quite steep and from the top one is given "a delightful prospect" of the surrounding land and sea, Mt. Desert Island, Penobscot Bay, the Camden Hills. The fir, spruce and pine which cover this hill cause it to appear at a distance of a very dark blue color, hence its most natural name.

Dr. Chase, herself, in *A Goodly Heritage*, in describing Bluehill Bay, says: ". . . northward . . . at its extreme head rises the great hill, a landmark to mariners past and present and a suggestion to more travelled eyes of Vesuvius beyond the Bay of Naples."

The town of Bluehill, Maine, is located in Hancock County. The township was first known as No. 5, then for a brief time called East Boston by the early settlers. The plantation name was Newport and at the time of its incorporation in 1789, it became the sixty-second town in the District of Maine.

Bluehill was first settled in 1762, near "Fire Falls," where Bluehill Bay runs into a salt water pond. The pioneers were Captain Joseph Wood and John Roundy. In a petition sent in January, 1762, to the General Court of Massachusetts, these first settlers of Bluehill described themselves as "husbandmen" living near the towns of Haverhill, Beverley and Andover, "without land sufficient for themselves and sons." They humbly begged for a "considerable Tract of Unappropriated Wilderness Land and Islands as they shall find suitable in some place or places on the Sea Coast between Passamaquoddy Bay and the land near the Penobscot." Their petition, granted two months later, was delayed until such time as his Majesty's Royal Approbation "might be obtained."

But the two petitioners already mentioned, weary of waiting, came without permission and with no rights whatsoever, and they were soon followed by the others. The third family in the town was formed by the marriage of Captain Wood's daughter with Colonel Parker, who had served at the siege of Louisburg. The family of Samuel Foster was the fourth, and following them were Colonel Nicholas Holt, Ezekiel Osgood and Nehemiah Hinckley. Several citizens of Bluehill served in the Revolutionary War. Christopher Osgood, one of the first settlers, was at the Battle of Bunker Hill; Nehemiah Hinckley served throughout the war and was honorably discharged at West Point. Ebenezer Hinckley, born in Brunswick, settled in Bluehill in 1766, where he resided on the Neck. He was frozen to death on Long Island, Bluehill Bay, where he and James Candage, Sr., had built and owned a saw mill. Ebenezer probably was the ancestor of all the Hinckleys. Among other early settlers were the Carletons, Peterses, Candages and Hortons.

A Congregational Church was formed in 1772 and a Baptist

Church in 1806. Jonathan Fisher, already mentioned, was the first settled Congregational minister and served from 1796 to 1837. He was a remarkable man, of broad interests and unusual energy.

The first post office was established in 1795, and Bluehill Academy was incorporated in 1803.

The town was a thriving seaport in the middle of the nineteenth century; before that an industrial development had taken place. Within forty years of its settlement in 1762, it had several small mills including one that spun cotton yarn; the lanes and harbors were echoing all day long with the steady pounding of hammers and sledges in the shipyards and there was also mining of minerals, chiefly copper.

Deer Isle, 1789

Deer Isle was incorporated as the fourth town in Hancock County, and the sixty-third in the District of Maine. It derived its name from the great numbers of deer found in its forests in the early days. It included Deer Island, Little Deer Island and Eagle Isle.

The earliest settlements upon these islands were in the 1760's: in 1762, Michael Carney settled on the north shore of the island. Wm. Eaton of Haverhill started the first settlement in 1762, near the steamboat landing; then came John Billings of Lincoln, Massachusetts, to the head of Little Deer Isle. He removed to Sedgwick, but one of his sons continued his residence here. The Greenlaw brothers, five in number: Jonathan, Charles, Ebenezer, Alexander and William, settled on Campbell's Neck in 1762. They were from Scotland. They removed to Nova Scotia during the Revolution, but two of Jonathan's sons later returned and settled at Deer Isle.

Among the other arrivals of that decade were the Torreys, Haskells, Dunhams, Sellers, Hoopers and Marshalls. About 1768 Mark Haskell arrived, probably from Gloucester, Massachusetts, with his sons, Ignatius and Solomon. They were shipbuilders, saw mill owners and real estate traders, and Ignatius came into a large property at the death of his father. This made him the most promising man in the community. He built a meeting house entirely at his own expense and sold the pews later to anyone who wished to contribute.

The first arrivals on Deer Isle came without benefit of legal title of any sort. They built rafts and floats to cross the Reach and set about clearing land and building homes; they enacted laws and organized churches and helped in the battle against the wilderness. The flow of new settlers was slowed by the Revolution, but never completely stopped. Massachusetts recognized the rights of all settlers on Deer Isle to one hundred acres of land as of January 1, 1784, upon payment of thirty-nine shillings to cover the cost of the survey. Those arriving after that date could purchase up to one hundred acres at a dollar per acre.

On March 24, 1788, the General Court called upon the larger islands and new townships settled upon the Penobscot River and eastward of it to assign their reasons why they did not apply for articles of incorporation. To remedy the inconveniences experienced by these people owing to the remoteness of the courts from them, the government was disposed to divide the County of Lincoln, as soon as there were towns enough from which jurymen could be legally drawn. Hence the call which so generally awakened the inhabitants of the plantations that within a period of some fifteen months, about twenty towns were incorporated. By 1789 there were enough settlers at Deer Isle to warrant its incorporation also.

During the Revolution, the warships of both England and the United States were active around Deer Isle, and in the War of 1812, several naval skirmishes are recorded as having taken place there.

Gouldsborough, 1789

Gouldsborough, the sixty-sixth town to be incorporated in the District of Maine, was originally granted to Nathan Jones, Francis Shaw and Robert Gould of Boston, who immediately settled it with lumbermen from Portland, Saco and vicinity. The town was called Gouldsborough in compliment to Robert Gould, one of these grantees. It is situated between Frenchman's Bay and Gouldsborough Harbor. Francis Shaw, Jr., born in Boston, July 28, 1748, went to Gouldsborough in 1770-71 as agent for the proprietors. He was a staunch patriot, much engrossed in the Revolutionary War, and in 1775 was captain of the Gouldsborough militia. In 1776 he made and ratified a treaty with the Indians on the St. John River, and as a private, he was a member of Captain Daniel Sullivan's company for the protection of Frenchman's Bay in 1780. He died in 1785. His son, Robert Gould Shaw, the great Boston merchant, was born in Gouldsborough on June 4, 1776; he and his brother were sent to Boston to an uncle for schooling in 1789. In 1793 he returned to Gouldsborough to care for his interests there, but after three summers the property was sold to Wm. Bingham, and Shaw became a merchant in Boston.

The first white man in our present town of Gouldsborough, as far as we know, was Nathan Jones of Weston, Massachusetts, who had been surveying land on Mt. Desert for Governor Bernard and sailed across the bay to find land for himself in 1762. The township was run out by Jones and Frie in 1763. Jones interested two Boston merchants, Robert Gould and Francis Shaw, who explored the township that year and in 1764 obtained a grant of the township under the usual instructions and limitations. Jones had one-eighth of the town and built a saw mill or one-half of one, the first in the town. Immediately after the completion of his purchase in 1764-65, he began the erection of mills on the Frenchman's Bay side and in 1768-69 moved his family there and carried on the business, until Shaw and Gould who had bought a part of the township and saw mill, started their settlement in 1764-65 and sent Francis Shaw, Jr., there as an agent in 1770-71 for all parties. Jones later moved to what is now Cherryfield.

The harbor was fine, the country beautiful, lumber abundant, but the soil was poor. Settlers were sent here, however, and farms were cleared, houses and mills built. The names of some of the original settlers were Robert Ash, —— Fernald, Tristram and Richard Pinkham from Boothbay, who built a tide mill and afterward moved to Steuben, Benj. Glazier and Ichabod Willey, who removed to Narraguagus before 1771. Nathaniel Denbo or Densmore, —— Goodwin, —— Tracy, Tobias Allen, Thos. Hill, Benj. Bickford, John Gubtail, Asa Cole, Isaac Patten and Daniel Tibbetts were early settlers. The Revolutionary War put a stop to all business and the settlers were destitute. After the war, operations were again begun, but lasted briefly. Francis Shaw, Sr., died in 1784 one year before Francis Shaw, Jr.

At the first town meeting held in Gouldsborough, April 4, 1789, the following officers were elected: Nathan Jones, Esq., moderator; Wm. Shaw, clerk; Dr. Benjamin Alline, treasurer; Thomas Hill, Samuel Libby and Eli Forbs, selectmen and assessors. Thomas Hill was constable and collector; Nathan Jones, Samuel Libby and Benj. Godfrey, surveyors of roads; Thomas Hill, William Shaw and Abijah Cole, surveyors of lumber; Wm. S. Jones, Clement Furnald and John Gubtail, Jr., fence viewers; Benjamin Ash and John Gubtail, Jr., deer reeves; Dr. Benjamin Alline, sealer of weights and measures and Peter Godfrey, sealer of leather.

Under the Bingham administration, General David Cobb came as agent and removed to Gouldsborough Point in 1796. The records show he was taxed a poll tax of twenty-eight cents that year. He conceived many plans to promote the interests of both proprietors and settlers. He hoped to found a city at Gouldsborough Point. The location was superb. Large wharves and store houses were erected, miles of streets were laid out in all directions up in the country, and some were built, as his diary shows. Ships sailed for England and the West Indies loaded with lumber and returned loaded with the products of those countries. The city did not materialize however. Enterprise and push were elsewhere, at Ellsworth, at Machias and up the Narraguagus. General Cobb lived in Gouldsborough for more than twenty years. He held the positions of Chief Justice of the Court of Common Pleas, major-general, Senator from Hancock County from 1801 to 1804, lieutenant governor, 1809, and President of the Executive Council, 1805-08, 1812-14, 1816, 1817. He moved to Taunton in 1820. For nearly twenty-five years he was the foremost man in eastern Maine.

Sullivan, 1789

Previously New Bristol, or No. 2, one of the David Marsh townships laid out by Samuel Livermore in 1762, Sullivan was incorporated in 1789 and named for Daniel Sullivan, one of its first settlers. Sullivan was born about 1738 in Berwick, son of John Sullivan, a schoolmaster in that town. His brothers were Governor James *Sullivan of Massachusetts; Major-General John Sullivan, Governor of New Hampshire, and Benjamin, a British officer lost at sea before the Revolution.

The early settlers came to our present Sullivan about 1762-63, because of its rare opportunities for lumbering and trade, which were carried on until the outbreak of the Revolutionary War. Among the early settlers who came then besides Sullivan were Bean, Prebles, Simpson, Gordon, Blaisdell, Card, Johnson and Hammond. The grant given to these newcomers was not ratified by the king as requested, so many returned to York; later, in 1803, the settlers were confirmed in the possession of 100 acres each by Massachusetts, on the payment of $5.

In 1776 Daniel Sullivan was commissioned as Captain of the 2nd Company, 6th Lincoln regiment; he immediately organized the company and built a sort of garrison or blockhouse near his residence.

The heads of families in Sullivan in 1790 are listed in the census of that year. At that time the town included our present Sorrento or Waukeag Point. Waukeag was the Indian name for seal.

At the first town meeting held in 1789 at the incorporation of the town, the following officers were chosen: moderator, Ebenezer Bragdon; clerk, Thomas Moon; treasurer, Captain Paul Simpson; selectmen and assessors, Jabez Simpson, John Bean, Agreen Crabtree; to lay out roads, Asa Dyer, John Preble, William Crabtree; surveyors of land and roads, Wm. Wooster, Agreen Crabtree; collector of taxes, Jabez Simpson.

Six additional men were elected as surveyors of roads; four, as surveyors of boards; five, as tithing men; and four, as hog reeves.

The monument to Captain Daniel Sullivan is in the cemetery near Highhead on Waukeag Point.

Trenton, 1789

Formerly No. 1 of the six second-class townships granted by Massachusetts in 1762 or 1764, Trenton was ceded to Paul Thorndike and others in 1785. The first English settlement known was in 1763, when Stephen Hutchinson, Ephraim Haines, Roger Googins and others came to the place. Before this, there were French settlers at Trenton and Oak Points. Thompson and Alley's islands are within its jurisdiction. It was incorporated in 1789 and named in honor of the Battle of Trenton, New Jersey, a memorable conflict of the Revolutionary War, fought on the 26th of December, 1776. Trenton, Maine, lies north of Mt. Desert Island, between Union River Bay and Jordan's River. The occupation of the people, aside from agriculture, is connected with the sea. Before 1870 Trenton had embraced the whole peninsula between Union River Bay and Frenchman's Bay, but at that date it was divided and the eastern half incorporated as Lamoine, to which area Captain Isaac Gilpatric came in September, 1774. When Trenton was incorporated in 1789, it contained about three hundred people. It is separated from Mt. Desert by Jordan's River, a branch of which is salt tidewater that stretches a league and a half into the town.

Among the heads of families included in the census of 1790 of Trenton Town (including Township No. 1, East side of Union River) are Ephraim, Parley and Peter Haines, Robert, Samuel and Marten Killpatrick, Roger and Thomas Googins, Solomon, Ebenezer and Meltiah Jordan, John and John Murch, Jr., James, Isaac and George Lord, Benj. Wiggins, Nathaniel, John and Wm. Jealouson, Edw. Berry, James and Thos. McFarland, Edward Hodgkins, Wm. and James Hopkins, John Harding, Silas Coolidge, Jacob Foster, Elisha Whitaker, Edmund Black, Joseph Bark, Farrington **Farrell**, James and Nathaniel Smith, John Springer, George Haslem, Samuel DeBeck, Job Anderson, Edward Sinclair, Thomas Hapworth, John Green, Jonas Farnsworth, Jesse Dutton, Joseph Morrison, John Tinker, Joanna Beal, Joseph Card, Theodore Jones, Henry Maddox, Robert Milliken, Wm. Fletcher and Joseph More.

In 1797 the town clerk was Perley Haynes; the selectmen, Jacob Foster, Perley Haynes and James Lord.

Mt. Desert, 1789

The first permanent settlement was made by the English. Abra-

Top: West Gouldsborough from Beech Hill. Town House is on the hill right of center
Bottom: Main Street, Bucksport, looking west from in front of the Merrill Trust Company Bank in the 1890's

Top: Eastern S.S. Co. "Penobscot" aground at Bucksport
Bottom: Bucksport Fire House in 1856

The man sporting the derby was a "traveling man." Bucksport

Top: Winter hay being sleighed on the frozen Penobscot River, 1874. Looking toward Prospect Ferry next to Fort Knox, opposite Bucksport
Bottom: Many and of various makes were the cars that used the Penobscot River ferry between Bucksport and Prospect
Opposite: The Old Tannery, originally the Blodget Tannery, on Franklin Street, Bucksport. Inactive since around 1959. The main tanning was skivers

J. B. Bradley & Co. (J. B. Bradley and William Ross), Carriage and Sleigh Manufacturers and dealers in harnesses, Bucksport

ham Somes came in 1761 and built a house near the head of the sound which bears his name. James Richardson came the same year. When the present town of Mt. Desert was incorporated in 1789, it borrowed the original name of the island. Among the villages included in the town are Northeast Harbor, Seal Harbor, Somesville and Otter Creek.

Some of the other early settlers were Stephen Richardson, a year or two after James, at Bass Harbor, Christopher Bartlett on Bartlett's Island, Israel Bartlett at Pretty Marsh. Other early settlers were Ebenezer Higgins, Daniel Rodick, Ezra Young, John Tinker, Josiah Black, Amaziah Leland, Levi Higgins and Thomas Richardson.

A petition from Mt. Desert in 1768 for protection against hay thieves was signed by Abraham Somes, Andrew Tarr, James. Stephen, Thomas and Elijah Richardson, Benjamin Stanwood, Stephen, Daniel and Daniel Gott, Jr. These last three were doubtless from Gott's Island. Some of the early settlers at Pretty Marsh were Ephraim Pray and Ephraim Pray, Jr., the Widow Eaton and Reuben and George Freeman.

Bucksport, 1792

The 79th town incorporated in Maine was called Buckstown, in honor of Colonel Jonathan Buck. In 1817 the name was changed to Bucksport. It was township No. 1 which had been conditionally granted with five others by the sovereigns William and Mary in 1762 to David Marsh of Haverhill, Massachusetts, and his associates. It was confirmed by the General Court in 1764.

The first settlement was started that year, where the village now is, by Colonel Buck, an emigrant from Haverhill, and his associates who moved thither with their families and built a saw mill and two dwelling houses. The place was called by the Indians "Alamasook." James Sullivan, the historian, speaks of Jonathan Buck as a very worthy man in whom the people of Penobscot had great confidence; he never deceived nor defrauded anyone and was popular with the Indians as a trader. He died in 1795. In personal appearance he was a thin, spare man about 5 feet 10 inches in height with a countenance very expressive of his thought, a Roman nose, large black arching eyebrows, and dark penetrating eyes. He was a man of iron temperament and will. He would not turn from what he thought right; an ardent patriot, he freely sacrificed all his property and barely escaped with his life from the hands of the British soldiers when Castine was taken in 1779. Jonathan Buck, Jr., was one of the most prominent men for many years in the management of the affairs of the town. As Justice of the Peace, he acted as judge in all petty cases of

Top: Fire on Main street, Bucksport
Bottom: Ladies' tennis team. Bucksport, 1880

law in this and adjoining plantations. He was the first Representative to the General Court, and Deacon of the First Congregational Church under the Reverend Mighill Blood.

In August of 1762 Colonel Buck, James and Wm. Duncan, Richard Emerson and Wm. Chamberlain had begun the survey of the town. Laughlin McDonald and his son, Roderick, from Greenock, Scotland, arrived and took up lots the next year. In 1766-67 Asabel Harriman, Jonathan Frye, Benjamin Page, Phineas Ames and others settled according to the condition of the grant which gave to each actual settler 100 acres of land.

The story of the settlement of Bucksport is the story of the settlement of the whole Penobscot Valley. Fort Pownal had been built below it in 1759 and was a protection to settlers. Its truck house became a trading house for dealing in fur with the Indians. As soon as the fort was garrisoned, the English settlements crept slowly up the river. The occupations of the first families at Bucksport were fishing, hunting, trapping and trading.

Many of the soldiers employed in the building of the fort had returned to Massachusetts, and the report they gave of this goodly land excited at once a spirit of immigration. Already there were several settlers on the Penobscot River, and townships were granted on certain conditions upon application. The first white inhabitant was Joseph Gross, who had been a soldier at Fort Pownal and afterward made a permanent settlement at Orland. After Colonel Jonathan Buck built his mill in 1764, he built a house and a small building near the water for a trading house. Asabel Harriman, of whom mention has already been made, was from Plaistow, New Hampshire. Like many of the first settlers, he was a mighty hunter and a bold, adventurous man. In 1775 there were twenty-one families in Bucksport, No. 1, and twelve in Orland, No. 2 The spring was dry and cold, there was little corn and grain of any kind grown on the Penobscot River and little or no sale of wood or lumber. The General Court recommended two or three bushels of grain be sent and sold for a moderate price in wood and lumber. Colonel Buck was appointed almoner. He was also in charge of Fort Pownal. He had built the first saw mill and the first ship on the river, and in 1776 organized a military company of fourteen soldiers as there were only fourteen in town liable to military duty. This "army" marched to the Castine peninsula to join the Penobscot Expedition in its unsuccessful attack on the British.

After the American retreat from the siege of Castine in 1779, the British ship of war, "Nautilus," anchored in Bucksport Harbor

Top: This long building was a rope walk, the home of "Castine Line," on Pleasant Street, Castine.
Bottom: Bar Harbor, 1874 or 1875

26

and, landing a crew of men, burned the town. The inhabitants fled through the woods to the Kennebec and to Massachusetts.

Colonel Buck's family was conveyed to Major Treat's, two miles above Bangor, and later joined him in Haverhill. In 1784, when the settlement was renewed, he returned and rebuilt the house and saw mill. The first preacher was Reverend John Kenney, who came in 1795. In 1796 it was "voted to build a meeting house on the parsonage lot 28 by 32 feet, one story," but this was dismissed at the next meeting. In 1803 the town raised $300 for the support of preaching, the first since 1797; the Reverend Mighill Blood (Dartmouth) became the first settled minister.

A post office was first established in 1799. The town grew raipdly; *The Gazette,* one of the first newspapers in Maine, was successfully printed there for six years. In 1801 Buckstown was one of the largest towns in the eastern section of the state. In 1804 Jonathan Buck was the first Representative to General Court. The first bank in the Penobscot Valley was established here in 1806. In 1814 the inhabitants suffered in common with many others the loss of their vessels and were under British power for eight months.

Castine, 1796

Castine, which was early settled and early incorporated, was named in honor of the Frenchman, Baron Vincent de St. Castine, who resided upon the peninsula where the town of Castine is now located, from about 1667 to 1697. He was a man of illustrious connections and noble extraction. He had come to Canada in 1665 in command of a regiment of French soldiers and at the close of the war settled upon the peninsula in 1667. Here the Plymouth Colony had established a trading post in 1626. Here were the headquarters and fort of D'Aulney, the Frenchman, from 1640 to 1651; and during the greater part of this period, the fort was often the scene of conflict between him and La Tour, rival proprietors, the first a Romanist, the latter nominally a Huguenot.

In 1674 the place was taken by a Flemish vessel commanded by Captain Jurriaen Aernoots.

Castine was separated from Penobscot and incorporated as a town in 1796. Castine's historian, Dr. George A. Wheeler, wrote:

> The first permanent settlement of our present Castine was commenced in 1761 under the name of Maja-bagaduce or as it was more commonly written, Majorbiguaduce. The first settlers were Paul and Caleb Bowden or Booden, as the name

Top: Bar Harbor Village, 1881. The few years have made a big difference.
Bottom: Green (now Cadillac) Mt. Railway 1883-93

28

was then spelled, John Connor, Andrew, John, Joshua, Reuben and Samuel Veazie, Thomas Wescott and Jeremiah Witham. The next year Andrew Webber came and took up a lot. In 1766, Andrew Clark and Abraham Perkins came. In 1772, Solomon Avery, Samuel Veazie, John Douglass, Reuben and Daniel Grindle and in 1773, Frederic Hatch were added to the number.

Twenty-three persons with their families settled in Maja-bagaduce the first year and the same number more in 1762. Between that time and 1784, eighty-four more were added, among them being John and Joseph Perkins whose numerous descendants still remain.

After the Revolution, Colonel Johonnet was the business founder of Castine, merchant, justice of the peace, exporter of lumber and importer of West Indian rum and other goods. John Lee was Castine's second notable citizen, coming about 1784, collector in 1789 and town clerk, 1787, town treasurer, from 1796 for many years. He was the largest land holder on Penobscot Bay, he owned saw mills and had large business interests. Mark Hatch was here in 1771, a merchant mariner and ship builder, one of the most influential citizens of Penobscot and Castine.

The British garrison was stationed in Castine from 1779 to 1783 and again for a year in 1812.

Bar Harbor, 1796

Bar Harbor, on Mount Desert Island, takes its name from the harbor with its Bar Island, which is directly in front and to the left of the town. The town was settled in 1763. It was taken from the northern and eastern parts of Mount Desert and incorporated under the name of Eden in 1796. Williamson says that the name Eden was given on account of the beauties of the place. This is the most accepted version, but Varney states: "The name was probably adopted in honor of Richard Eden, an early English statesman." In 1918 this name was changed to Bar Harbor.

The petitioners for the incorporation of the town in 1796 asked that the name Adams, in compliment to Governor Samuel Adams of Massachusetts, might be bestowed on the new municipal corporation. This was not granted; instead the town was incorporated under the name of Eden. Since the word is an old British river-name identical with Eden Water and Afton Eden, it may have been given for that reason, rather than those presented above.

Most of the men who made the real settlements on the island came from western Maine, Arundel (Kennebunkport) or Harpswell;

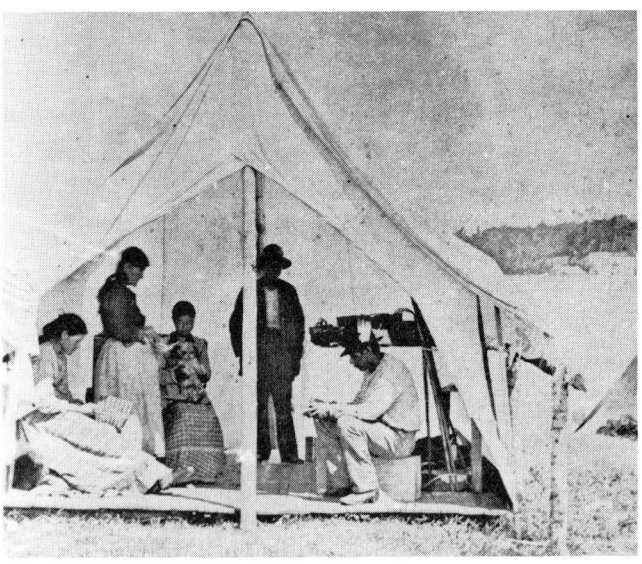

Top: First hotel, the Agamont House. T. Roberts, Proprietor, 1855.
   Bar Harbor
Bottom: Nineteenth-century Indian camp on present Athletic Field.
   Bar Harbor

some were from Cape Cod or Cape Ann, some from Nova Scotia. These early settlers moved away from the rough sea side of the island. It was they who at last made a true settlement. According to Eben Hamor, there were eleven families in Eden before 1770. At Bar Harbor proper were Israel Higgins, Daniel Rodick and old "Uncle Ebeneezer" Salisbury; the last named was an emigrant from Nova Scotia, who settled first in a log house where the Newport Hotel stood later, before moving to Salisbury Cove. At Duck Brook were Ezra Young and his wife. At Hull's Cove in 1762 were Elisha Cousins, Levi Higgins and John Hamor, who had moved to this place directly from their homes; also Simon Hadly and Timothy Smallage were here. At Leland's Cove was Amariah Leland. At present the villages of Hull's Cove, Salisbury Cove and Indian Point lie within the township of Bar Harbor.

At Town Hill, West Eden, in 1790 Gideon Mayo had settled and in the first decade of the nineteenth century, Prince, Thomas and James Mayo were there; by 1818 Ephraim, Joseph, David and Samuel Higgins, James and William Hamor and Thomas Knowles had arrived.

The first meeting house at Hull's Cove was of the Baptist denomination and was built before 1797 by the proprietors, a large high-posted building. The wall pews were square and elevated about ten inches above the center pews and had seats on three sides. The pulpit was very high with a door for an entrance. There was a great deal of moulding work around the inside, and it was a very grand and sacred place. At the town meeting of 1797 it was "Voted that the Selectmen should purchase the meeting house for the town of the proprietors," with other actions concerning preparations for its use.

Orland, 1800

While Orland, Hancock County, is not named for its earliest settler, it is said by tradition to have been named from an experience of the first settler, Joseph Gross. On his arrival in 1764 he found on the shore of the river an oar, from which the name Oarland (Orland) is derived. This township was No. 2 of the grant given to David Marsh and his associates in 1762. For a considerable period of time, the place was called Alamasook, and then Eastern River. It was incorporated in 1800. It is at the head of Eastern River, fifteen miles west of Ellsworth.

Ebeenezer Gross came in 1765 and Joseph Viles in 1766; the latter erected the first frame house which was used for plantation meetings until 1800, when a schoolhouse was built. The first road was

Top: Mason's Mill. East Orland
Bottom and opposite: Aspects of lumbering. At one time, according to Albert A. Davis, in *History of Ellsworth, Maine,* Ellsworth, the shire town of Hancock County, ranked as the second largest lumber shipping port in the world.

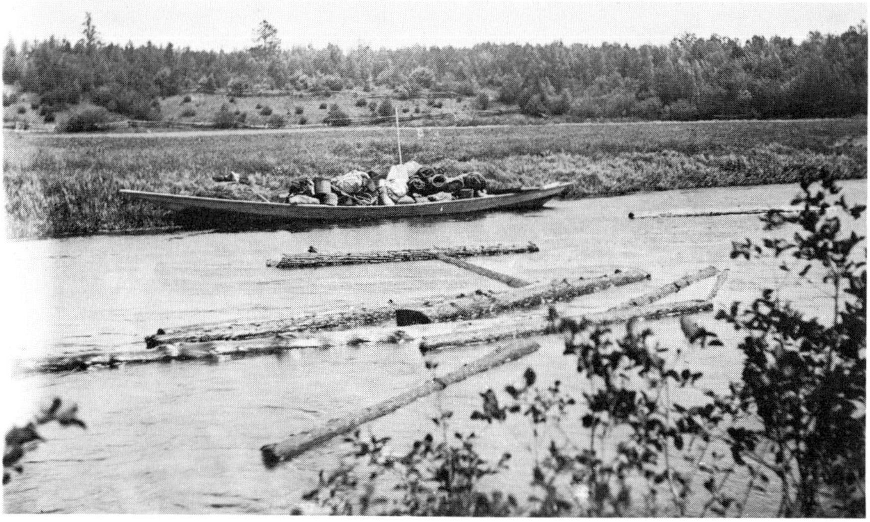

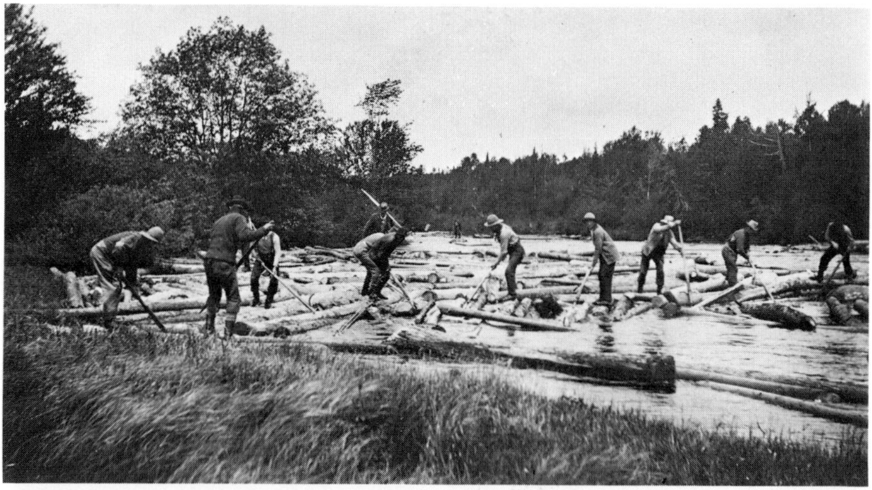

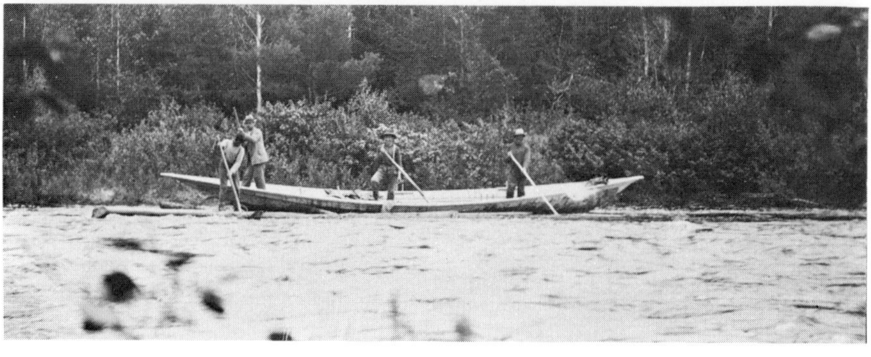

Main Street from Bridge Hill. An early picture of Ellsworth

Top: The Ellsworth schooner "Mary C. Hale," 539 tons. Built by I. M. Grant, 1875. Only one coaster sailed in and out of Ellsworth in 1830. By 1853, 149 sailing vessels of all descriptions were owned in whole or in part.
Bottom: The schooner "Henrietta A. Whitney" formerly the "E. & I. Oakley," originally built elsewhere, but rebuilt at I. M. Grant yards for Whitcomb & Haynes and an Ellsworth vessel in 1888. Destroyed by fire at Eastport, summer of 1924.

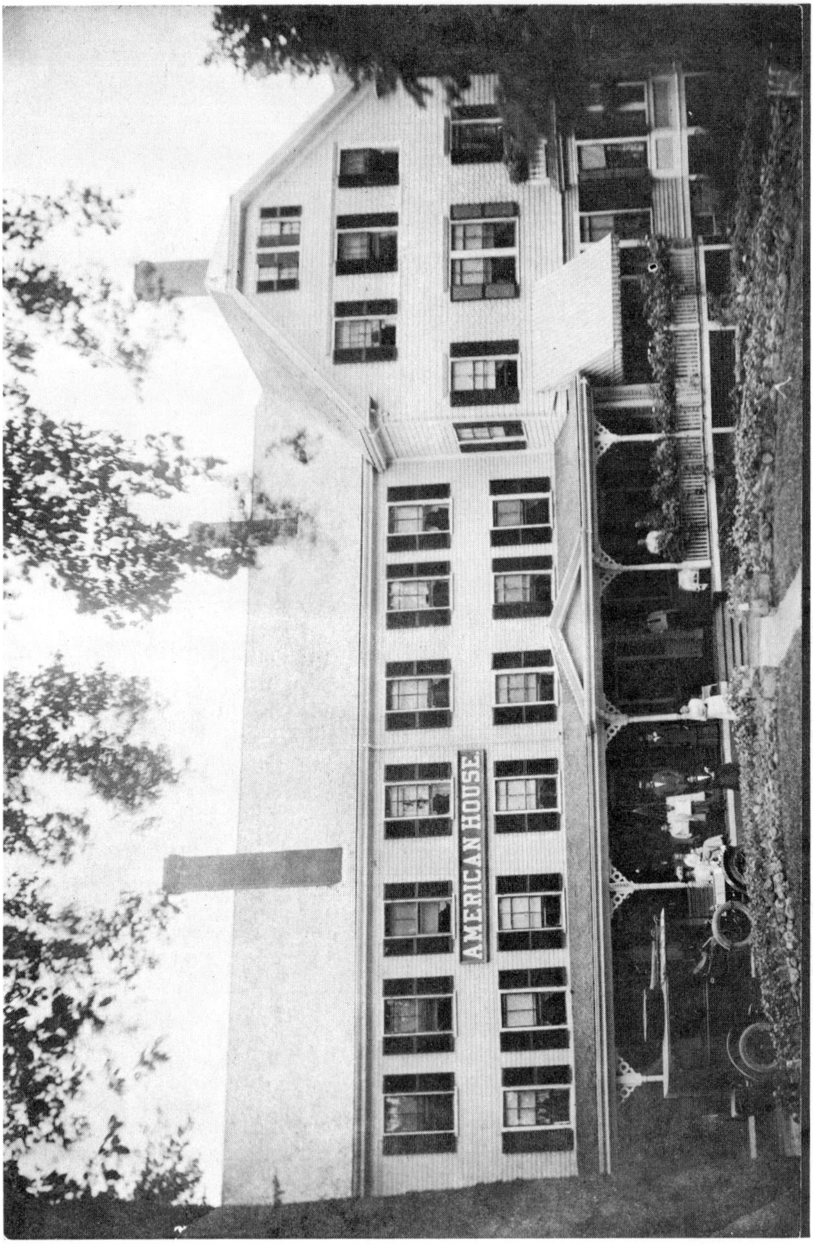
AMERICAN HOUSE

Top: The Ticonic No. 4, Ellsworth Falls, according to historian Davis, "a first-class 10-inch Button, made in 1862" came to Ellsworth from Massachusetts in 1866. Fire engine muster contests were a favorite New England pastime, during which each engine played a perpendicular and horizontal stream, to see which could pump water highest and farthest. Ticonic's best horizontal was 223 ft. 4" at Ellsworth, July 4, 1889.
Bottom: Main Street, Ellsworth, 1891

Opposite:
According to A. Davis, building of the American House was begun in 1836 by Benjamin Jordan, who sold out to Joshua Hathaway when it was nearly completed. The latter conveyed it to Benjamin Tinker.

37

Top: Ross Taylor, driver. One of the last of the John M. Hale coach line. First six-passenger coach and four began to run in the early 1830's.
Bottom: Main Street parade, July 4, 1894. Ellsworth

Top: George P. Smith and Merrill R. Head entered partnership in men's clothing in 1913.
Bottom: Taken from the west side of the Main Street bridge before the Union River flood of May 2, 1923, carried it away. Dirigo Theater is building on the left, and post office is on the right.

laid out in 1771 by John Hancock and Samuel Craig. The first saw and grist mills were built at Lower Falls by Calvin Turner in 1773.

A large number of settlers came from Boston between 1767 and 1780, among whom were John Hancock (the most noted), Samuel Keyes, Samuel Soper, Calvin Turner, Asa Turner, Humphrey Holt and Samuel Craig. Robert Treat was appointed an agent by the proprietors to run out lots, which he did at Upper Falls in 1774. He started to build the first saw mill at Upper Falls that year. In 1781 Ezekiel Harriman and Peter and Asa Harriman moved from Plantation No. 1, now Bucksport, and each took up a settler's lot. James Ginn came from Brewer and took over the mill of Robert Treat and carried it on until 1797. He also built a brig and two schooners at Upper Falls. In 1797 Robert Treat sold his mill and lot to John Lee of Castine.

In 1773 an old hunter named Michael Davis had come from Concord, Massachusetts, and taken up a lot three miles from any settler. He had built a log house on a ridge of land and hunted for a living, as there was a great quantity of game. He had lived alone until James Smith, Nathan Hancock, John and Joshua Gross and Andrew Craig moved in and took settlers' lots that were run out in 1780. This land, with the exception of that of James Smith, was owned by the sons of the first settlers and was considered the best land in the plantation at this time. Jacob Sherburne took up a lot at what is now Sherburne Point. He was hired by the proprietors to lot the plantation in 1791-1793. At this latter date the first county road was built and the first bridge across Eastern River; the county furnished sixty pounds and the plantation fifty pounds.

In 1800, the year the town was incorporated as Orland, the first schoolhouse was built. It was also used as a meeting house and town house. Joseph Lee was the first town clerk in 1801. In 1811 John Lee of Castine brought the first chaise to town. Joseph Harriman, born in 1790, says: "When I was a boy, it was a dense wilderness and the greatest town in the county for all kinds of lumber, but by 1870 it had about all been marketed. The first settlers, especially the children, must have suffered for want of bread. Salmon, shad and alewives in the rivers furnished much of the diet." He also states that Plantation No. 2 was granted to the proprietors Wm. Dall, Nathan Snelling, Robert Treat and others, then living in Boston, on condition that they should have so many settlers in so long a time, when the grant would be given by the General Court.

Ellsworth, 1800 (City, 1869)

Benjamin Milliken, said to be the founder of the present city

Top: Yard of the Ellsworth Foundry & Machine Works. The foundry collapsed during freshet that preceded the flood, caused when the new Brimmer Dam of the power company gave way. The old Steam Laundry building, storehouses of the Farmers' Union, Dirigo Theatre, and many yachts also lost.

Bottom: Taken from west side of the river after bridge went out. Collapsed building left of center is the theatre.

Top: Ellsworth business district aflame, May 7, 1933
Bottom: After the fire. A path of destruction 500 yards wide. Two hundred
  buildings, including two churches, the Town Hall, 25 stores, 60 dwellings,
  and many smaller structures, including summer boats, were lost.

of Ellsworth, was an enterprising man who had been many times "at the eastward" and came to Ellsworth, or Union River, as it was then called, from Scarborough in 1763. His daughter Abagail accompanied him. He started the building of a dam and mill, probably a tide mill, and it was a failure. Then he and his brother, Thomas, built a dam at the head of the tide and their mill at its east end, in Surry. The mills paid little. Milliken sent lumber in rafts around to Castine for the British to use in the building of Fort George. Other saw and grist mills soon followed.

Among the next settlers from Richmond's Island, Biddeford, Scarborough and Falmouth were: Meltiah Jordan, Benjamin Joy, Colonel Jones, George Lord and Nathaniel and John Jellison. Others soon followed. Twenty years after its settlement, the township had a population of 992. The first minister was Reverend J. Urquhart, who came in 1785. The Reverend Peter Nourse was ordained in 1812. For thirty-two years the township was known as Union River Settlement and Union District; and, from 1795 to 1800 it was known as Bowdoin and New Bowdoin, probably in honor of James Bowdoin of Massachusetts. According to the petition of 1798, the inhabitants were anxious to try the name of Sumner, but this was not granted because there was already a town by that name in Oxford County. The name was finally decided by the General Court and was given in honor of Oliver Ellsworth, an able judicial leader, who was a Massachusetts delegate to the National Convention in 1787 for the adoption of the Constitution of the United States. Ellsworth comprised No. 7 of the "Ten Townships"; a part of Township No. 6 was annexed to Surry soon after 1820, but was re-annexed to Ellsworth in 1829. Ellsworth became the shire town of Hancock County in 1838 and a city in 1869.

Ellsworth is noted for its beautiful buildings; among them is the old Congregational Church of which it is said: "this parish has given more great men to the State and Nation than any other church of its size in Maine, perhaps in New England"; the Black House, where John Black, an Englishman, "finely educated in the elegant attainments peculiar to the higher classes in the land of his birth" was land-agent for the Bingham interests, and the Public Library, built in 1817 by Meltiah Jordan for his son, Benjamin.

Surry, 1803

The town of Surry was Township Number 6 in the grant of the first-class townships to David Marsh and 359 others in 1762. These townships were to be located severally, six miles square, in a regular contiguous manner between the Penobscot and Union rivers.

The grantees bound themselves to certain conditions, among them the settlement within each township of sixty Protestant families within six years after obtaining the King's approbation, and the building of as many dwelling houses, at least eighteen feet square; the fitting for tillage of 300 acres of land and the erection of a meeting house and settlement of a minister. There were reserved in each township one lot for parsonage purposes, another for the first settled minister, a third for Harvard College and the fourth for the use of schools.

Surry was first settled about 1767. Pioneers were from Cheshire, New Hampshire, Newbury, Massachusetts, and Berwick, Maine. The first English settlers were Symonds, Weymouth and James Flye. Andrew Flood, Sr., one of the early settlers, came from Cheshire, New Hampshire, and erected a log cabin on the shore of what is now East Surry. In March of 1791 he was chosen the first juror from Surry to serve at court in Castine. Moses Hammond, the first trial justice receiving his appointment from Governor King, settled near "the Floods." In 1784 at "No man's Cape," as Newbury Neck was called, there were a number of settlers from "Old" Newbury, Massachusetts. The Clarks, Treworgys, and Youngs are descendants of men who settled in Old Newbury.

Other early settlers were John Patten, a Mr. Hopkinson, Wilbrahim Swett, Matthew and James Ray, Samuel Joy, Isaac Lord, Hezekiah Coggins and Leonard Jarvis.

The last named and his brother Philip, who were brothers of Boston merchants, began to buy up land as early as 1770 from the original grantees and from the state, and by 1800 were the largest landholders in Maine except for the Bingham estate. Leonard Jarvis represented the eastern division in Congress from 1831 to 1837.

A letter from John Ross of Surry, now Ellsworth, to General David Cobb, at that time President of the Massachusetts Senate, concerns the name of the town of Surry. Ross was a Scotchman who had come to Ellsworth about 1790, and after the purchase of the Bingham estate had become an agent for General Cobb.

The letter is dated "Union River 25 January 1803." After speaking of the weather and a few news items, he continues: "Our plantation has sent a petition to get incorporated the name I cannot like very well, nor am I alone in my opinion, could you get it called Kent or Surry or indeed any short name of your choice, twould be more acceptable."

Evidently his desire was carried out, for the town became Surry after the English town which he suggested. The name was even shortened, since the spelling of the English town is Surrey.

Brooksville, 1817

The early history of the town of Brooksville is largely included in that of Castine and Penobscot. James Rosier was an "English Gentleman" who accompanied Captain George Weymouth to this country in 1605 and wrote an account of the voyage which was printed in London. Rosier's name is perpetuated by Cape Rosier, the headland in the southwest corner of Brooksville in Eastern Penobscot Bay. The suggestion is made, however, in the *Wayfarer's Notes* that Cape Rosier was not named for the old navigator, since there is no evidence that Rosier went as far east as Penobscot Bay. An old fisherman says that Cape Rosier was named for its abundance of roses.

Upon Henry's Point, near Oliver Bakeman's, the British erected six gun batteries in 1779.

The first settlers were John, Thomas and Samuel Wasson and David Hawes, Revolutionary soldiers. They found three squatters already in possession: a Mr. Roax, Eben Leland and Arch Haney. About 1780 Wm. Roax and Elisha Blake settled upon the cape. The first white child born within the present town limits was Mary Grindle. Of the Wassons, Thomas was a fifer and served three years in the 15th Massachusetts Regiment; John, also a musician, served three years in Colonel Bradford's Regiment, while Samuel was a drummer. John Bakeman, Sr., was first at the Neck and also at Cape Rosier, where he is said to have erected mills. Samuel Marble came in 1769; John Condon was at Buck's Harbor prior to 1780, while Jonathan Holbrook, or his son Prince, built mills at Goose's Falls — probably after the Revolutionary War. Others among the petitioners to the town of Penobscot, later citizens of Brooksville, were Elisha Hopkins, Noah Norton, Thomas Kench, Ben Howard, John Bakeman, Jr., John Condon, Edward Howard, Malachi Orcutt, Jacob Orcutt and John Redman.

A resumé of the life of John Brooks for whom the town was named offers many interesting facts. He was the ninth governor (1816-1820) of Massachusetts and a soldier, born at Medford, May 3, 1752, the son of a farmer. He was educated in a country school and indentured as a medical apprentice to Dr. Simon Tufts. He was always interested in the drilling and marching of British soldiers on his visits to Boston. He located at Reading as a physician and received his commission as major in the army soon after the battle of Concord and Lexington. In 1777 he was appointed Lieutenant Colonel of the 8th Massachusetts Regiment. At the Battle of Saratoga, he stormed and carried the intrenchments of German troops. In Colonel Trumbull's picture of the "Surrender of Burgoyne," Colonel Brooks ap-

Top: Jones Corner Grocery, dating back at least to 1840's, associated with pioneer Walker and Perkins families. Brooksville
Bottom: Old Carding mill. Brooksville

WEST BROOKSVILLE, ME.   Old Bray House

NORTH BROOKSVILLE, MAINE.   Old Bridge and Mill Race

Top: The John Bray House at West Brooksville is claimed to
have existed since Revolutionary days.
Bottom: Old bridge and millrace. North Brooksville

pears in a prominent position. He was at Valley Forge, where Baron Steuben was introducing his new system of military tactics, and Colonel Brooks was ordered by Washington to help bring it into general use. Later, after the troops had encamped on the Hudson, he was employed by Steuben to further assist in the introduction of this new system. Brooks enjoyed the confidence of Washington. He held many important political positions after the war. He toured Maine in 1818 and died in 1825.

Franklin, 1825

Located on Taunton Bay, a prolongation of Frenchman's Bay, this town was named for Benjamin Franklin.

There are several ponds in Franklin, with streams furnishing considerable water power. It had, in 1880, nine lumber mills, two grist mills, a tannery and three granite quarries. The material wealth of the town is mainly in its water power and granite. Nearly one third of the hay in Franklin is on the salt marshes whence it is raked and boomed in as the tide flows. Cranberry culture has received some attention with successful results. Franklin is said to have shipped more spars, railroad ties and ship timber than any other town of its size in Hancock or Washington counties. Franklin was orginally Plantation No. 9. It was first occupied by the French at Butler's Point. Moses Butler and Mr. Wentworth came in 1764 and are supposed to have been the first English settlers. The next were Joseph Bragdon, Mr. Hardison, Mr. Hooper and Abram Donnell. On Butler's Point are apple trees more than one hundred years old.

Hancock, 1828

The town of Hancock is located in the southern part of Hancock County. It was settled by pioneers in 1764 and incorporated as a town in 1828, formed from parts of Sullivan, Trenton and No. 8. It was christened Hancock in honor of Governor John Hancock, who served from October 25, 1780, to February, 1785, and from 1787 to October, 1793, the date of his death. Perhaps it would be more correct to say that the town took its name from the county, which had been named to compliment the governor when it was incorporated.

The early post office in this area, before Hancock became a town, was called Sweetland.

The town lies between Taunton Bay on the east and Skilling Bay on the west. Two of its streams, Kilkenny and Egypt, have sufficient power to turn mills. The villages are Hancock and North and South Hancock. There have been mills for manufacturing staves, shingles and long lumber, and one producing staves and short lumber. Other manufactures have been boots, shoes, wagons and sleighs. In the earlier days the inhabitants, especially those of the Neck, were largely engaged in Grand Bank fishing. The pioneer settlers were Oliver Wooster, Agreen Crabtree, Thomas McFarland, Thomas Rogers and Joseph Googins. In 1766-68, came Philip Hodgkins, Reuben Abbot, Thomas Moon and Richard Clark.

Cranberry Isles, 1830

These islands take their name from a marsh extending 200 acres on the largest island. They were included originally with Mt. Desert as a town, but were set off and incorporated separately in 1830.

The first English settler within the limits of the town was John Robertson, who located upon the island which bears his name in 1761-62. Some of these islands were included in the grant to John Bernard in 1785, and some to DeGregoire and his wife in 1787. The property of the latter was sold to William Bingham, on July 9, 1796: Great Cranberry, Little Cranberry, Sutton or Lancaster, Baker and Bear Islands are in the group.

The first settler on Great Cranberry was David Bunker who is said to have moved away; Benjamin Spurling, who was from Portsmouth, New Hampshire, and the ancestor of most of the families by that name in Hancock County, spent his life here. He sold a lot for sixty pounds to Joseph Wallace of Narraguagus. William Nickels was an early settler, but moved to Narraguagus; his heirs were granted a lot laid out by John Peters. Jonathan Rich, who had come earlier from Marblehead, moved from Mount Desert to the island previous to 1790, and John Stanley also arrived early.

On Little Cranberry Island, Samuel Hadlock, Sr., who had first located on Mount Desert Island, where his buildings had burned, was an early comer. He was born at Marblehead and died on Little Cranberry Island in 1854. On Baker Island, William Gilley of Mount Desert was the first settler. William Moore from Sutton's Island settled on Bear Island and died there at the age of seventy-five. Joseph Lancaster from Sullivan was first on Lancaster or Sutton's Island. Isaac Richardson went to this island from Mount Desert and died there at the age of eighty-three.

The first board of selectmen at incorporation consisted of Samuel Hadlock, Enoch Spurling and Joseph Moore.

Aurora, 1831

Aurora takes its name from the goddess of dawn who, ac-

A beautiful example of church architecture in Maine. The old church of Great Pond, Aurora

cording to Greek mythology, opened, with her rosy-tipped fingers, the gates of day, so that Apollo might start the chariot of the sun god upon its daily round. Aurora was one of the "Lottery Townships" and was organized as Plantation No. 27 in 1822. For a brief time it was called Hampton. It was incorporated as the town of Aurora in 1831.

Its first settlers were four brothers, Samuel, Benjamin, David and Roswell Silsby, who took up their abode in the township about 1805. During the winter of that year Samuel, with his brother Wendell, left Ackworth, New Hampshire, for Portland with a load of produce. From there the journey was made on foot through Bath, Rockland, Camden and Bucksport. From this last point the way was made on snowshoes to the present town of Amherst, where his brother, Captain Goodell Silsby, awaited him. From this plantation he proceeded to the township, now Aurora, cleared land and built a log cabin into which he moved in 1812. Jesse Giles was the next cómer.

Aurora is situated on a branch of the Union River, on the "Air Line" road, twenty-four miles from Ellsworth and twenty-five from Bangor. The roads run over the hardwood hills which were principally occupied by the first settlers, and afford pleasant views. The woods are generally of pine, spruce and hemlock. The present village inn was formerly a stagecoach stop. Just beyond Aurora, the Air Line passes over the whaleback, an alluvial ridge with an elevation of from two hundred to three hundred feet..Vast tracts of woodland stretch along either side. Some fifteen miles beyond Aurora and about three miles from the Air Line are the beaver colonies and dams on the Narraguagus.

Amherst, 1831

Amherst is situated on Union River, in the center of Hancock County. This town was a part of the Bingham Purchase. It was set off from the plantation of Mariaville in 1822 and incorporated in 1831. It is said to have been named for Amherst, New Hampshire. Settlements were begun about 1805. In that year Captain Goodell Silsby came in and in 1805-07, his parents arrived and took lots now known as the "Old Silsby Place." Before the close of 1808 a half-dozen other families had taken up lots: those of Moses Kimball, Asahel Foster, Jesse Gils, Joseph Day, Judah West and Elisha Chick.

There have been saw, grist, clapboard and shingle mills as well as a large tannery here. The latter used hides principally from South America and Mexico. The Union River divides the town diagonally into two nearly equal sections. The principal hills are known as the Springy Brook Mountains. Amherst has been remarkable for its improved domestic cattle. The tannery at Amherst, owned by Buzzell and Rice, was of great advantage to the people residing in the northern part of Hancock County.

Amherst, New Hampshire, received its name in compliment to Lord Jeffrey Amherst who came to America in 1758 at the suggestion of Wm. Pitt. As Major-General, he was in command of the troops who captured the fortress of Louisburg on Cape Breton Island. In 1760 Amherst was made Governor-General of British possessions in North America, in which position he remained until 1763, when he returned to England.

Waltham, 1833

Situated near the center of Hancock County, Waltham is on the eastern side of Union River. The town was carved out of Mariaville in 1822 and incorporated in 1833, taking as its corporate name, Waltham, from Waltham, Massachusetts. This township was part of No. 14, Middle Division of Bingham's Penobscot Purchase, now in Hancock County. It was first settled in 1804, when all travel to the present town was by canoe or boat on the Union River. The first settlers were George Haslam, Lebbens and Eben Kingman, Caleb Kingman, Samuel Ingalls, Joseph Jellerson, Wm. Jellerson, Richard Cook, Ebenezer Jordan and Joshua Moore. These pioneers left their families at Ellsworth, went up the river and located their lots. They felled trees, built log houses and the next spring, 1805, moved their families in.

Webb's Brook, the outlet of Webb's, Scammon's, Abram's and Molasses ponds, affords a valuable water power; a mill was built there for the manufacture of staves and shingles. The settlement was increased every year by other families moving there: John Fox, Chas. Jones and Hugh Twynham, who came later from England, were among them. The principal business in the winter was making shingles and clapboards. They floated their lumber on rafts to Ellsworth, from which it was shipped to Boston. The first saw mill was built in 1832 by Captain Stephen G. Woodward, Hugh Twynham and Increase Jordan.

Otis, 1835

Situated in the northwestern corner of Hancock County, Otis is bounded on the north by Penobscot County and on the south by the city of Ellsworth. It has many lovely sheets of water which empty into Union River or some of its branches. Much attention is given to lumbering.

When incorporated in 1835 it was named in honor of an original proprietor, Joseph Otis.

This lovely town was first occupied in 1805; the first settlers were Isaac Frazier, N. M. Jellerson from Union River, later Ellsworth, James Gilpatrick from Lamoine and Allen Milliken from Mt. Desert.

Mariaville, 1836

Mariaville is situated in the middle of the western side of Hancock County. It was organized as a plantation in 1820 and originally was called Bingham for the great landholder, William Bingham of Philadelphia, whose first purchase was the 1,000,000 acres in Hancock and Washington counties, including the lottery lands. The present town of Mariaville was included in this purchase and received this name at its incorporation in 1836. For years all "up river" (the Union River) was known as Mariaville, but the town has been reduced to its present unshapely outlines by the taking off of Aurora, Amherst and Waltham in 1822.

The names of the pioneer settlers were Mr. Fabrick, Seth Alcott, B. and D. Eppes, James Hapworth and Elisha Goodwin. Tilden was once a part of Mariaville. William Bingham had two daughters, very gay and accomplished, one of whom, Anne Louisa, married Alexander Baring, afterward Lord Ashburton. The second, Maria Matilda, was distinguished for her three marriages into the nobility of France and England. It was for her that the town was named.

Dedham, 1837

Situated in Hancock County, Dedham was named for a Massachusetts town and was originally a part of Township No. 8, which also included Otis. It was incorporated under its present name in 1837, the name being suggested by Reuben Gregg who had formerly lived in Dedham, Massachusetts. The colony was for years known as New Boston, and the inhabitants were accused of "putting on airs." It was settled about 1810 by Nathan Phillips. The Massachusetts town of Dedham had in turn received its name from an English town.

There are ten considerable peaks in the town, of which Bald Mountain, "Old Bald," is the highest. Between these peaks are about as many ponds, also some excellent farms and orchards. Some fine water powers are on the outlets of the ponds where a grist mill, a carding mill, saw and shingle mill and a large tannery have been located. The present Club House at Lucerne-in-Maine (Phillips Lake) was the old "Half-way House" on the Bangor-Ellsworth stagecoach route, the building now much remodeled. It was built just after the War of

1812. Nathan Phillips, already mentioned as the first settler, came from Bellingham, Massachusetts, to Eddington Bend, then to Brewer, and from there to Phillips Lake. He built his first log cabin near the shore, but later another log cabin on the hill, near the site of the Club House.

Other pioneers followed, treking their way into this rude wilderness. There seemed to be a general exodus from the western part of the state to this town, including the Billingtons, Burrills, Blacks, Cowings and others. Two brothers, Asa and John Burrill, came to Dedham in 1826 from China, Maine. William, Asa's son, said he was fourteen years old when he came to Dedham, and he had to walk all the way from China to lead the family cow.

Thomas Cowing and his family came from Lisbon in 1826. His son, Daniel, who at that time was ten years old, said he remembered coming by ox-team, taking a week to make the trip, and that his mother cooked up doughnuts enough to fill an old-fashioned churn, for them to have on the journey. Men like these carved farms from rugged hillsides, monuments to their daring and faith.

At the first town meeting in 1837 William Saunders was elected moderator; Elijah Devereux, town clerk; Caleb Stockwell, Perley Haynes, John Burrill, selectmen, assessors and overseers; Melzar Brewster, treasurer; Dominicus Milliken, William Jellerson, John Burton, constables; William Jellerson, Frederick Fry, Elijah Devereux, superintending school committee; Reuben Gregg, Frederick Fry, Daniel Burrill, surveyors of lumber; Frederick Fry, Perley Haynes, Josiah Burrill, Daniel Fields and George Blaisdell, fence viewers.

During the first year of Dedham's existence as a town, eight meetings were held in different places, evidently to accommodate residents in the several districts, and on account of the condition of roads and modes of travel. At the last meeting the census of the town revealed sixty-five heads of families in all.

Eastbrook, 1837

The writer of the *Eastbrook Centennial History*, Mrs. Josephine Butler, states that "the name of the town derives from the fact that the drainage of the southern half of the township flows into the east branch of the Union River"; or as Varney puts it: "The name is derived from the Eastbrook branch of the Union River."

The first permanent settlers came about 1800, and the town was incorporated in 1837. These first settlers were Joseph Parsons, Robert Dyer, Samuel Bragdon and John E. Smith. The first mill and the first frame house were built by Joseph Parsons. Francis Usher Parsons was the first child born in the town.

Among the early settlers listed above, Bragdon, himself a hunter and trapper, became the first permanent settler; Robert Dyer was the first to bring his family, in 1811.

As the settlers came, saw mills were needed to transform logs into boards for homes. The logs were taken from the clearings where fields were needed to raise corn for food. A grist mill was also needed, to grind the corn into meal. Joseph Parsons built the first saw and grist mills at the mouth of Scammon Pond. Thus lumbering and farming became the first industries. The Union River offered a way also for driving the logs from the northern part of the township to Ellsworth for manufacture. A second mill built at the foot of Molasses Pond, the Macomber Mill, made many soft-wood products: long lumber, staves, shingles and laths. Later hardwood products were manufactured.

Among the familiar names of those who followed the first comers and had a large part in the development of the town were Abbott, Billings, Bowden, Bunker, Butler, Ashe, Crimmins, Curtis, French, Googins, Jellerson, Kingman, Lowrie, Merchant, Piper, Potter, Springer, Scammon and Wentworth.

An abundance of sugar maples in certain sections of the town has resulted in the development of a maple sugar industry.

A church was not built until 1859-60.

Tremont, 1848

Tremont takes its name from three contiguous peaks: Beech Mountain and East and West peaks of the Western Mountains. The word Tremont is from the French *tre* and *mont* (mountain). Tremont was set off from Mount Desert and incorporated on June 3, 1848. under the name of Mansel, from Mt. Mansel, the name given to the mountain by Winthrop's company of emigrants to Massachusetts Bay in 1630, it having been the first land discovered by them in this country. On August 8th of the same year, the name was changed to Tremont.

This section of Mount Desert Island was included in the grant to John Bernard, the son of Governor Bernard, in 1785. Some of the early settlers in this section before 1808 were: Joshua and Wm. Norward, on the east side of Bass Harbor; Abraham and Thomas Richardson and Thomas Richardson, Jr., at Bass Harbor Head; Peter and Daniel Gott, Stephen Richardson and Benj. Benson, on the west side of Bass Harbor; Daniel Merry's heirs, on Lopers Point, and Enoch Wentworth and Wm. Nutter, in the vicinity of Duck Cove.

Brooklin, 1849

This town was formerly a part of Sedgwick but was set off

55

Top: Fishermen at Gott's Island, Brooklin
Bottom: Old cattle pound at Brooklin. Every Maine town had one in the nineteenth century.

from that town in 1849 and incorporated under the name of Port Watson. One month later, its name was changed to Brooklin. I am indebted to Mr. Windsor Bridges for the origin of the name: The two towns, Brooklin and Sedgwick, are divided by Salt Pond and Benjamin River, a tidal river, which are connected by a brook. It was because the line of separation follows this brook that the name Brooklin was given to the town.

The names commonly connected with the first settlement of the town are Black, Reed, Goodwin, Watson and perhaps Freethy who located at Naskeag Point. Shadrach Watson sold merchandize at Naskeag in 1762.

Naskeag Point is the far outer tip of the neck that is included in the township of Brooklin. This point is frequently mentioned in documentary history and may have been occupied at a time and by people now unknown. Revolutionary history narrates the courage and irregular methods of fighting of William Reed and his neighbors when, in 1778, the British sloop, "Gage," prepared to land men here.

The first officers of the town in 1849 were David Hooper, moderator; David Carlton, clerk; Azor Cole, treasurer; Humphrey Wells, Andrew Seavey, and Stephen Cousins, selectmen.

Verona, 1861

This town is an island toward the mouth of the Penobscot River off Bucksport and Orland. It was anciently called Penobscot Island then Wetmore's Island and Orphans Island.

In 1763 there were three families on the lower end of the island and no settlers above on the river. After the Revolutionary War, the heirs of the Waldo Patent claimed it and the General Court granted their claim. The island was owned by the wife of Wm. Wetmore, a granddaughter of General Waldo and daughter of Samuel Waldo of Falmouth. Wm. Wetmore was a lawyer in Castine; he may have come as early as 1789. He was the only lawyer in Castine ever elevated to the degree of barrister, an honor which required the recipient to appear in court in wig and gown. He was born in 1749, graduated from Harvard in 1770 and settled in what is now Castine. He is said to have been Judge of Probate in Hancock County.

It was to Wm. Wetmore that on May 18, 1879, Samuel Waldo of Boston sold one half of this island; and on May 2, 1790, Lucy Waldo of Boston sold a quarter of the same for $300. Widow Sarah Waldo sold him the remainder of the island.

It was called Orphans Island for a while because it was all that remained for General Henry Knox, who owned a large portion of the Waldo Patent, to bequeath to his orphan grandchildren.

When the town was incorporated in 1861, it adopted the name of Verona, an ancient Italian city in Venezia, whose splendid monuments rendered it attractive to travelers.

"The Wayfarer," commenting on the "outlandish name of Verona," says that like some others, it has no significance, nor any relationship to any person or ancient name in the vicinity.

Under the census of 1790, the following are given as living in Orphan Town (Verona): Syrenus Collins, Bazilah Hopkins, Peleg Hearsy, James Scott, Wm. Nickerson, James Cunningham, James Buckley, Wm. Mace, Moses Blaisdell, Moses Sanders, Caleb Merrill, Frederick Hames, Isaac Webber, Benj. Lillie, Eleazer Walker, Eliphalet Perkins, James Abbott, Wm. Grout, Wm. Pomroy, Joseph York, John Crocker, Benj. Rawlins, Thos. Cummins, Jonathan Blake and Samuel Richards.

Lamoine, 1870

This town in Hancock County was set off from Trenton and incorporated in 1870. It was named for an early French settler, De LaMoine, who at one time owned a large tract of land west of Skilling's River. A colony of French made a transient settlement at Trenton Point at an early date, and two of the colonists remained permanently. According to the statement of the Honorable Wm. King, Maine's first governor, the first settlement at Lamoine was made in 1774 at Gilpatric's Point by the individual whose name it bears, and the French came subsequently to this first English settler.

Captain Isaac Gilpatric whose name is retained at "the Point" came from Biddeford with six sons and two daughters and a son-in-law, Edward Berry, from Londonderry, New Hampshire.

Winter Harbor, 1895

Deriving its name from the open or free harbor upon which it is located is Winter Harbor. Its sheltered harbor has never frozen.

The village of Winter Harbor is situated within the mouth of Frenchman's Bay on the mainland of the State of Maine, in the old town of Gouldsborough, from which it was separated in 1895. The water is deep to its shore and the formation is such that many vessels have found safe anchorage there. It was settled in the early 19th century by a race of sturdy fishermen whose descendants compose the population of today and retain the characteristics of their ancestors.

At Lower Harbor one of the first settlers was a colored man named Frazier who owned the salt works there. Another, John Frisbee, came from Portsmouth, owned a large fish stand and some vessels, a part of a fleet engaged in the West Indian trade. His son, George, was a sea captain.

In 1820 Stephen Rand of Boothbay came to Winter Harbor, where six families were living at that time. He built a house at the head of the sand beach. Joseph Bickford was then living in a two-inch plank house at the east side of the village. His sons were Jacob, John and Benjamin.

Another of the old settlers was Andrew Gerrish, who lived in a house built of six-inch hewn timber. The partition was also of timber. The other family in the house was that of Francis Coombs from Fox Island. A. Sargent lived at the east end of the village and Dr. J. Rolf on the west side. The people were occupied in coastal trade and fishing.

Among the captains of the mackerel fleet were Captain Solomon Pendleton, who was lost on his return trip from Bay Chaleur in 1855; Captain Nathaniel Grover and Leonard and Peleg Tracy.

The captains who later sailed to foreign ports, either the West Indies or across the Atlantic, were Captain Nathan Hammond's sons, Montgomery, Thomas and Wilson; Captain A. J. Gerrish and Captain J. B. Foss, who made several voyages to Africa.

Sorrento, 1895

Situated in Hancock County, this town is located on Frenchman's Bay and offers a vista of mountains and sea which makes it, in the minds of many travelers, the counterpart of its namesake, the Italian city on the Bay of Naples. It was formerly a part of Sullivan, but was set off and incorporated in 1895.

Cadillac was the French lord here in the seventeenth century. Douaquet, as it was then called, was one of the seigneuries established by the French authorities at strategic points. The Indians frequented Sorrento with their furs, since access was easy through many streams and rivers and over short portages.

The first English families of Waukeag Neck, now Sorrento, were Benjamin Ash, James and John Bean, Ebeneezer, Moses and Joseph Bragdon, Richard Downing, Samuel and William Ingalls, John, Nathaniel and Samuel Preble, Daniel Sullivan, Jabez Simpson, John Urann, John White and Benj. Welch.

Stonington, 1897

Stonington was a part of the town of Deer Isle and called

Green's Landing, 1880. The village that grew to be Stonington

Green's Landing until 1897, when it was incorporated under its present name. This was bestowed upon the new town because here are located quarries of granite, the products of which are suitable for building purposes. The early history of the town is included in that of Deer Isle. Nathaniel Kent, in 1768, built a grist and shingle mill which was a tide mill, as many of our early coastal mills were.

Job G. Goss was the first to begin operating the quarry. There was no village there at the time he purchased the land from David Thurlow on an outlying island. Thurlow Island is about two hundred yards from Stonington.

There were four great granite quarries in 1910, which had developed after 1870. Since the latter date, the quarries at Stonington have been the greatest in the country. G. S. Goss, a pioneer in the granite business, started the first at Green Head and afterward developed quarries on Crotch and Moose Islands.

Ryan and Parker on Crotch Island developed a second important quarry which furnished large quantities of stone for New York buildings. Rogers' Quarry at the settlement had its beginning about 1900; and Bien Venue Quarry on Crotch Island, developed some five or six years later, furnished stone for the building of the Museum of Fine Arts in Boston.

The village of Oceanville is a part of Stonington. Here a Baptist society was organized in 1807 by members of the Sedgwick Church.

Swan's Island, 1897

Swan's Island in Hancock County is thirty miles south of Ellsworth and five miles southwest of Tremont, with which it has communication. Its population in 1940 was 452. The island was named for Colonel James Swan who bought the Burnt Coat group from Massachusetts in 1786 and built a large mansion on the island which now bears his name. The house is no longer standing. Burnt Coat Harbor is the chief port of Swan's Island. The name is a corruption of Brulé-Côte or Burnt Hill which Champlain gave the island in 1604.

Colonel Swan was born in Fifeshire, Scotland, and came to America in 1765. He was a member of The Boston Tea Party, an ardent patriot, a merchant, politician, soldier, author and intimate friend of Washington and LaFayette and other Revolutionary leaders. He was a volunteer and aide-de-camp to General Warren at the Battle of Bunker Hill, and captain of the artillery in the expedition which drove the British fleet from Boston in 1777. Despite hardship and privation he succeeded in colonizing the Burnt Coat group of islands. In 1808 he was arrested for debt and confined in a French prison. Since he was not responsible for the debt he remained in prison twenty-two years rather than pay it. When Louis Philippe ascended the throne, Swan was released, but he died three days later.

Residents on Burnt Coat Island in 1790 were David Smith, Moses Staples, Joshua Grindle, John Rich, Wm. Davis, David Bickmore and Isaac Sawyer.

Southwest Harbor, 1905

Southwest Harbor, on Mount Desert Island, is the site of the first attempt of the Jesuits to found a permanent settlement in New England in 1613. The area was set off from Tremont and incorporated as a town in 1905. Its name is descriptive not only of its geographical location upon the island, but also of its harbor, or haven. When Governor Sir Francis Bernard came to inspect Township No. 2 of the David Marsh townships which had been given him, he planned his metropolitan center at Southwest Harbor and the location of his mill sites near by, deciding which marshes would provide hay and other details. He gave Abraham Somes and James Richardson pledges, written on birch bark, that he would let them stay on the lots they had settled.

More impressive than the lakes of Mount Desert Island is Somes Sound which is sometimes described as the only true fjord on the Atlantic Coast. It nearly cuts the island in two with its seven miles of crystal blue water winding up between meadows and hills. It was at the head of this sound that the island's first settlers made their homes in 1761. The neighborhood bears the name of Seawall, because the shore is a long natural wall of boulders which have been cast up by the sea. Southwest Harbor is on the western flank of Somes Sound, diagonally opposite Northeast Harbor. Though it is the oldest point in settlement, it is the newest town by incorporation. Another village included in Southwest Harbor is Manset which is thought by some to perpetuate the name of Sir Robert Mansell who came into possession of Mt. Desert in 1620.

Abraham Somes of Gloucester came down in 1761 by boat and cut a load of staves at the head of the sound which now bears his name. He apparently liked the spot and told others, for he came back with his family and lived on his craft until he could establish a home for them. The next settler was James Richardson, also from Gloucester. When Sir Francis Bernard was at Mt. Desert in 1762, he wrote in his journal under the date of October 7: "We went on shore and into Solmer Somes log house; found it neat and convenient though not quite furnished and in it a notable woman and four pretty girls neat and orderly." Mr. Somes was one of the principal men of Mt. Desert and one of the first selectmen elected on April 6, 1789.

INDEX OF CITIES AND TOWNS

Including secondary list of villages and hamlets*

Towns and cities (**)	villages, etc.	page
Amherst *see also* Mariaville		51
Aurora		49
	Great Pond	
Bar Harbor		29
see also Mount Desert	*Eden*	
	Hull's Cove	
	Indian Point	
	Salsbury Cove	
Bluehill		4
	Bluehill Falls	
	East Bluehill	
	North Bluehill	
	Seaville	
	South Bluehill	
Brooklin		55
see also Sedgwick	*Haven*	
	Naskeag	
	North Brooklin	
	West Brooklin	
Brooksville		45
see also Castine	*Cape Rosier*	
Penobscot	*Harborside*	
Sedgwick	*Herricks*	
	North Brooksville	
	South Brooksville	
	West Brooksville	
Bucksport		23
	Bucksport Center	
	Buck's Mills	
	East Bucksport	
	North Bucksport	
Castine		27
see also Penobscot	*North Castine*	
Cranberry Isles		49
see also Mount Desert	*Baker's Island*	
	Bear Island	
	Islesford	
	Little Cranberry Island	
	Sutton Island	
Dedham		53
see also Otis	*Green Lake*	
	Phillips Lake	
Deer Isle		12
	Dunham's Point	
	Eagle Isle	
	Great Deer Isle	
	Little Deer Isle	
	North Deer Isle	
	Reach	
	Sunset	
	Sunshine	
Eastbrook		54

* These villages, plantations, and hamlets which have never reached the status of towns are listed in italic under the nearest town (even if not mentioned specifically in the history thereof) as an aid to the tourist, at the request of the publisher and by permission of the author.